A PIECE OF CAKE

Mary Leunig was born in Melbourne in 1950 and was educated at various state schools. Diverted from art studies by her two children, she completed her Diploma of Art in 1975. She lives with her family in the Victorian country town of Daylesford. Between housework and the pub on Friday nights she 'draws pictures'.

Mary's first book, *There's No Place Like Home*, was published by Penguin in 1982.

A Piece of Cake

DRAWINGS BY

MARY LEUNIG

PENGUIN BOOKS

Penguin Books Australia Ltd,
487 Maroondah Highway, PO Box 257
Ringwood, Victoria 3134, Australia
Penguin Books Ltd,
Harmondsworth, Middlesex, England
Penguin Books,
40 West 23rd Street, New York, NY 10010, USA
Penguin Books Canada Limited,
2801 John Street, Markham, Ontario, Canada L3R 1B4
Penguin Books (NZ) Ltd,
182-190 Wairau Road, Auckland 10, New Zealand

First published by Penguin Books Australia, 1986

Made and printed in Singapore by
Kyodo Printing Co., Ltd

Leunig, Mary, 1950-
A piece of cake.

ISBN 0 14 009339 7.

1. Australian wit and humor, Pictorial. 2. Caricatures
and cartoons – Australia. 3. Home economics – Caricatures
and cartoons. I. Title.

741.5'994

SEED BELL
BUDGIE
SEED BELL

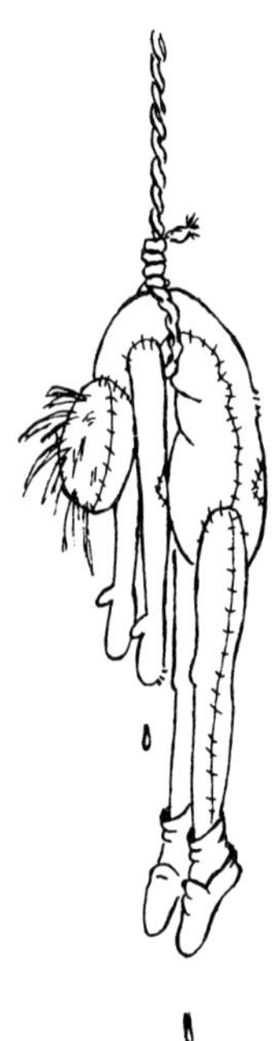

Mary Leunig

no!

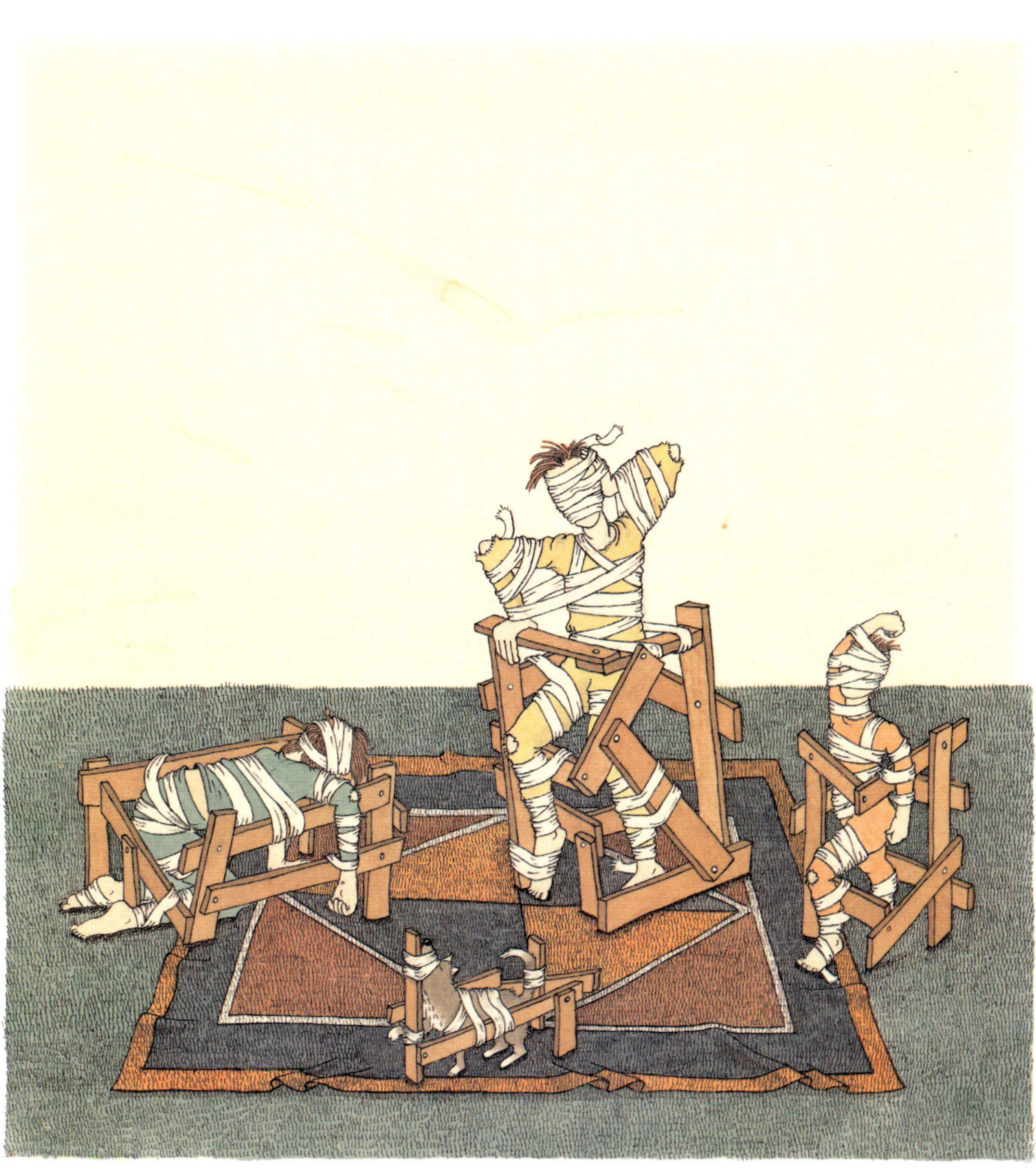

NATIONAL VIDIO CASSETTE RECORDER
AIR CONDITIONER
HITACHI
OPRA TAP WARE
APPLE COMPUTER
VULCAN SINK WASTE DISPOSER
TOSHIBA STEREO COLORED TELEVISION
POOL FILTER
AKAI VIDIO CAMERA
PAL

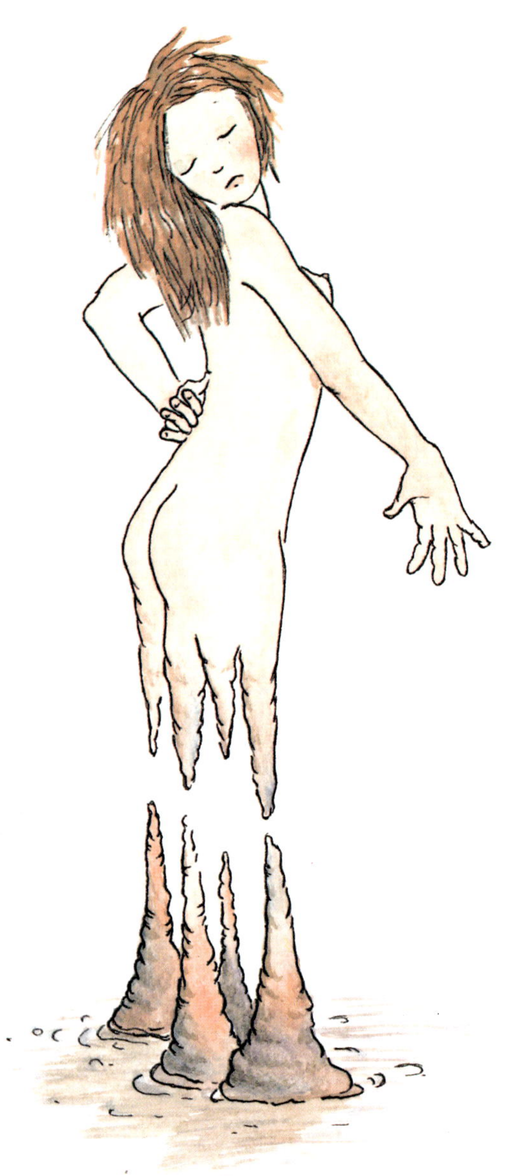

Mary Leunig

RIGHT
WAY

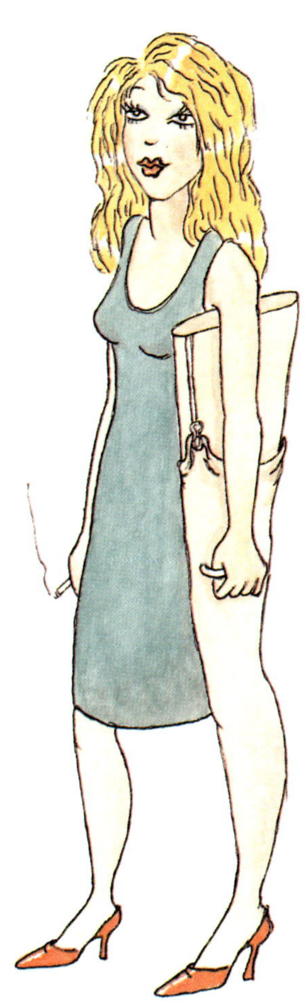

Mary Leunig

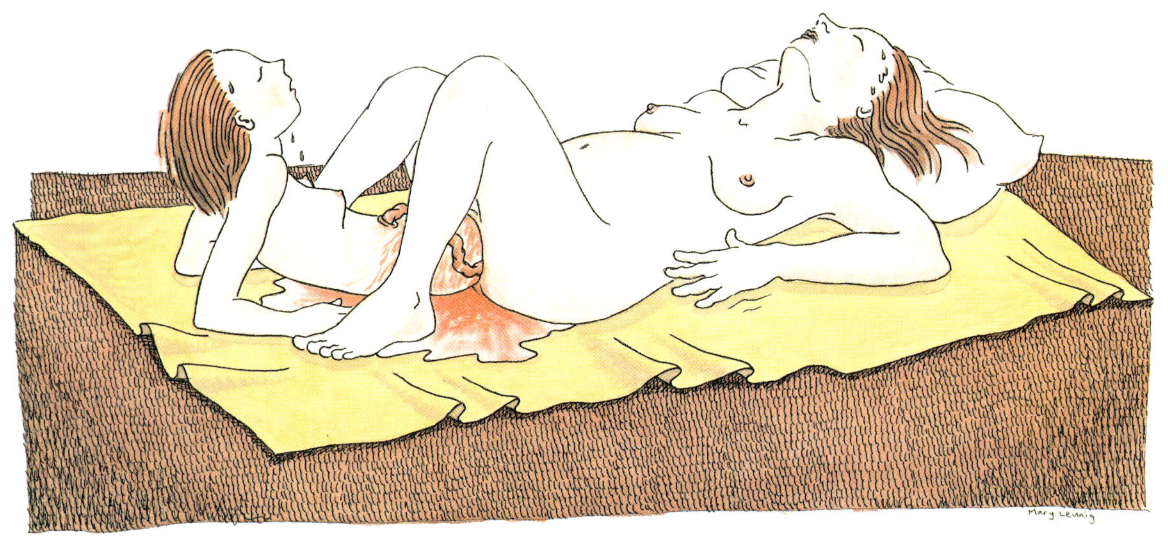

Mary Leunig

VIDIO HIRE
VIDIO HIRE

ROYAL-PARK
LAKE-SIDE
LARUNDEL
CLAG